Nothing but the Truth

The Things We Don't Talk About

Copyright

Published in Winter Haven, FL. Published by Horton International Ministries, Inc.

All inquiries should be addressed to:
hortoninternationalministries@gmail.com

Print 1 – Volume 1, May, 2021

ISBN: 9 780578 911267

From The Author

It has taken many years for me to write this book. I praise and thank God for getting me through all those years.

This book is where I open my heart, pour out my soul and reveal the deepest, darkest secrets that have permeated my life for some time. It is refreshing to be able to get it out.

"Nothing But the Truth" is not meant to hurt anyone but to let people know that the things you hear about actually happen in real life. The sexual abuse, the physical abuse, the emotional abuse, the tortures of life actually happens.

You may never know what a person is experiencing in life. As an individual, you may not know yourself what you are experiencing. My plea is that you read this book and recognize that there is help.

God is the vindicator. God is the help. If you can find a small, wee bit of faith to believe— that's right, **BELIEVE**, then you can be saved and relieved of the miseries of life.

Contents

Dreams and Nightmares

What a way to start off? Dreams and nightmares are what I most remember from childhood. My dreams were about places I had never been and places I had never seen. The dreams were pleasant dreams.

The nightmares were of snakes and worms crawling in the bed with me. I would try to suffocate and kill them with my blanket. I woke up screaming because of this nightmare that came over and over again.

When I screamed, my mother would come to see what was wrong. This is when she would find me standing on the dresser. I could not answer her questions about what was wrong, because I was still asleep. Here I am, standing on the dresser, fearing the snakes and worms, peeing as I scream. This nightmare was terrifying.

At that point, my mother would bring me into her bedroom to sit on the floor. Her thought was that I would feel safe in her bedroom. The reality was that I was fighting the snakes and worms there for the remainder of the night.

As dawn approached I would fall asleep. When I would wake up I would see shoelaces and cotton balls on the floor besides me. These were the snakes and creatures I wrestled with all night. Nightmare!

For me, walking in my sleep was a common occurrence. Once I found myself in the fireplace the next morning. Obviously, I was sleepwalking. My brother was there as well. I have no idea how I got into the fireplace.

In later years, my Mom told me about some of the adventures I had while sleepwalking. Once both my Mom and sister thought there was a burglar in the house before they realized it was me, sleepwalking.

Not only did I have nightmares and sleepwalking to my credit as a child. I also heard voices. At five years old, while walking to school I heard someone calling my name across the playground.

This was scary and strange. Of course, I didn't answer. However, even at five years old I believed in God and that He was watching over me. I have no idea where this thought came from, but I believed there was a God and He knew me.

My feeling, at that point, was that God was the sun. Since the sun seems to follow you wherever you go, in my mind I felt God (the sun) was always watching over me.

At primary school I was a quiet and withdrawn kid who didn't share the dreams and nightmares I had at home. As the dreams and nightmares became more frequent, I started to act out in school.

In First Grade I was reported to the principal by my teacher. Vividly, I recall being dragged to the principal's office, kicking and screaming to let me go. These actions led to my being placed into special education classes. Branded!

Some of our problems, I now realize, were brought on by the teachers who were not so nice. As I look back now, I feel some teachers were aggressive and aggravated me at times.

We moved a lot as a family so that different teachers, different styles, different adaptations and adjustments were a constant for me. It is difficult for me to remember all the schools I attended. Those early years were not the best years of my life. Neither were those great years for my brother when he was younger.

I have tucked the years between special education classes, primary school and elementary school in Detroit, Michigan delicately out of my mind. I choose not to remember any of these schools.

White or Not?

My complexion has been a source of trouble throughout my childhood.

One day my daddy came home drunk, as usual, and these girls beat me up in front of him. He didn't do anything because he looked like he was white as well. I wonder if it bothered him that people might mistake him for white, or the neighbors would sneer and turn up their noses because of his color. Well, that's where I got my complexion. My father's grandmother was white.

A girl in our apartment complex spit in my face and I beat her with a stick. This was all because she called me a "white bitch".

Over the course of growing up I had several fights around my complexion. This was a sore spot for me as I lived in a predominantly black neighborhood, went to a predominately white school for "bad" girls and lived a confusing live.

I always felt the necessity to protect myself from these name callings although I was proud of my father's heritage.

The complexion issue followed me from childhood to adulthood. My sister and I were looking for a job. We went to a go-go bar and both decided we didn't want to work there as we were not taking our clothes off. We got the newspaper and found this placed called Dance a Dime. It was a dance place where you wore sexy clothes, lingerie or whatever you want to be sexy.

The girls were sitting around the room. The guys bought tickets to give to any girl they wanted to dance for dimes. This seemed pretty interesting at the time.

We were different shades in my family. My sister was darker than me. The people at this dance hall thought I was white. When those white girls called me white bitch, I had to fight. So I had fights there as well.

Mostly older men were there. Some of the girls were prostitutes. This place got busted by the police several times. My sister liked the place because guys would come and give her $50 just to look at her. I didn't like this so much so I left; it was boring not my kind of place.

Acting Out

The one school I do remember is Goldberg Elementary on 12th Street, Detroit, Michigan. This is the school from which I would run home because someone wanted to fight me. My mother put an end to that. She said. "…if you come home one more time saying someone beat you up, then I'm going to beat you".

I knew from that point on I had to fight my way out of these attacks. My mother would beat me with an extension cord, a broomstick, a lamp cord, or whatever was close at hand that was not nailed down. You would not want to get beat by her!

As a kid I liked to hustle and one time in school I stole from a friend who was a very nice girl. I had no control over stealing during these years. My friend put down $5 and it was tempting to me, so I stole it. When she found the $5 was missing, she reported it to the teacher.

The teacher searched everyone in class, including me and didn't find the money on me. I got away with that. This was, naturally, encouraging to try other devious acts.

There was another time my brothers were fighting each other. One brother laid money on the dresser. I didn't know exactly how much money, but, I remember stealing it while they were fighting and he didn't notice it was gone. I got away again.

Some friends invited me to their house and I noticed that they had a piggy bank. So, I thought I would trick them into playing hide and seek. While they were hiding I went into the house, stole the piggy bank, opened it and took the money. I came out the house saying, "…ready or not here I come".

I put the money into a milk carton after removing it from the bank and later buried it in the ground. I couldn't sleep all night for thinking about something someone told me about burying money in the ground. They told me it would go deeper in the ground.

It was summertime and we weren't using overcoats. First chance I got, I dug up the money and hid it inside the house in a winter coat. I thought the money would be safe there but my sister, Sandra, found it in the coat pocket. Now, why was she digging in a winter coat pocket in the summer? Did she see me hide the money there?

At the time there was no food in the house, so Sandra bought food and candy for the house with the money she "found" in the coat pocket. When I discovered the money gone, Sandra explained she "found" money in the coat pocket and used it for food.

What could I say? I couldn't say the money was mine. I suppose all ends well since we now had food. So, I kept quiet all these years.

Adolescent Wild Days

I knew nothing about puberty, about menstrual periods or virginity. The girls at school asked if I was a virgin and I couldn't answer because I didn't know what that meant. They also asked if I had my period and I couldn't answer that either.

My mother did not tell me about life. When I asked my mother what's a virgin. She said, "none of your business just stay one."

After that if I came in the house with a smile or seemed to be happy, I was accused of having sex with a boy or doing something wrong. Around age 10 or 11, I started drinking. I drank any liquor, whatever I got my hands on. I started skipping school and running away from home.

My friend, Diane, and I were both in Special Education. We went to Inkster to visit with her Aunt and spent the night. During the night Diane let boys in a side door. Diane didn't care who touched her. As for me, I didn't want anyone trying to touch me or have sex with me.

I told Diane's aunt that she was sneaking boys and booze in the basement. She got in trouble, and we couldn't stay there another night. This is why, I believe, she set me up to be molested, at age 13.

I was molested by a 26 year old man who was married. This man beat me and raped me. I didn't feel anything as I turned myself off. I tuned it out. The end result, I didn't socialize with Diane anymore after that.

At age 14 my friend, Regina, and I ran away to the west side of Detroit, near Euclid and Woodward Streets. We were walking the streets with no place to lay our heads. We went to houses with boys and men, where they would let us sleep.

I can remember at one of these houses I was drunk and recall crawling around on the floor over the naked bodies of strangers. When I first woke up there was a strange man lying next to me. Yes, he probably had sex with me but, or course, I was drunk and couldn't remember.

Regina didn't want us to leave. But I wanted to leave. I felt very uncomfortable. We were doing all kinds of crazy things, like trying to rip men off who were drunk. Regina was using drugs and her boyfriend wanted us to turn tricks for him.

I had to beat him. No choice. I had to beat him. He hit me in the head with a glass ashtray and blood went everywhere; blood was over my coat.

I don't know how we got out of that one but we escaped. We went back home. The streets weren't quite that interesting and they were too dangerous.

I didn't have any friends as a young girl because when my friends would come over to visit my brothers would swap and molest them and they would not come back. It was embarrassing to have people around me in such a dysfunctional home.

My friend, Regina, was considered the bad girl in the neighborhood. They wouldn't touch her or molest her and we are still friends. Although we got in trouble frequently, running away from home, getting drunk, and having sex parties, we stayed friends.

A lifesaving episode with Regina was when we ran away to a different area of Detroit. We met up with some guys to party; drinking and having what we called fun. Yet, these guys were dangerous. These guys chased us down the street threatening to kill us because things were not going their way.

Regina and I ran for our lives and went into this apartment building. We ran knocking on doors for someone to answer and help us. Finally, an older couple allowed us in and saved our lives.

Once inside the apartment we could hear the guys outside saying, "…where did those bitches go?" We are alive today because they did not find us and eventually gave up the search. Why they were chasing us? I really don't recall but it probably had something to do with our end of whatever shady deal we were doing at the time.

Return to Inkster

I went to Inkster again with Regina. The popular song at the time was, "Runaway Child…running wild." A group of guys that Regina knew took us out in the boondocks. I have no idea where we were.

Fun turned to attempted rape. Isn't this natural? Isn't this what ultimately happens? Why didn't we see this coming? Regina gave in and I didn't (once again). My resistance ended in being beaten, clothes torn, thrown around and abused physically.

At this point the guy put a knife to my throat and said, "…bitch, if you scream I will cut your throat," and, as I prayed, the police came up and I screamed. I will call these guys Ice Cream and Tom, because I do not know their names. I told the police Tom threatened me with a knife and attempted rape. The police took everyone who was there to the police station.

As a runaway and because of my age, I didn't want to call my mother. I never should have run away from home. The driver of the car, Ice Cream, was not involved in raping us, so I asked him to call someone he might know to help.

Prayers answered. A woman called and pretended to be my mother and told the police to release me and Regina, as we were cousins to Ice Cream. We were all released with a court date on Monday.

The boys told us when we got back to the house that should we testify they would kill us and throw us into the Detroit River. I begged for my life and said, "I am not going to court". I pleaded that I would not testify. Instead, I would go back home to Detroit and never come back to Inkster again.

I did not go back there as a teenager. My son moved there and I have visited him as an adult, but never did I go back to Inkster again as a child.

The Change Starts

I went back home after this runaway to my dysfunctional family. At least, I would be alive.

When I went back to school the principal called me in and said I scratched up this girl. His question was did I use a knife? No, I didn't use a knife. I used my nails because she called me a white bitch in front of my friends. Expulsion from school was immediate.

There were times I would go down to Wayne State University. The students would leave their purses in the bathroom or sitting somewhere on a table. As a young girl, I would steal their wallets and or money. I was terrible like that (age 10-12).

I collected money in a cup for some girls who said they needed socks and panties. When they asked for the money I beat them and didn't give them a dime of the money I collected.

I had no control over stealing. It was like I had a love for money and would steal it every time I saw money. I always knew God and knew it was wrong for stealing. I would always say I'm sorry. But I just had no control.

Then I changed. What changed my thinking about stealing was when I dropped money in the bathroom and a girl scout found me to return the money I dropped. Wow, I thought to myself. People actually give money back to people when they know it doesn't belong to them.

Now, with a different attitude about giving and doing right there were several incidents where I was the one to give. I was in a restaurant and saw money on the floor. I picked it up and gave it to the gentleman sitting at the table. He said, "thank you. It's not mine but thanks."

At the grocery store I saw a lady fumbling in her purse and then saw her $100 bill on the floor. I picked it up and gave it to her. It wasn't mine and I was changing. Instead of stealing I was giving back because I knew it was wrong to steal. I thank God that I began to give back to people. This was a beginning of a change in my life.

At a time when my children were small I did some things that weren't good. I hit my children. I feel badly now. I didn't want to become the mother my mother was. My mother would beat me with an extension cord or anything she could find. I didn't want to be that kind of mother.

I began to put myself in time out. I would stop and think about the situation before I did anything about it. I asked my children as they became older did I ever do anything to hurt them. They said, "no, Mama." I asked them to forgive me if I ever did anything to hurt them. My kids said I never even hollered at them as my mother did to me. The kids feel they got away with a lot of things because I never wanted to beat them. Or have them hating me.

My Dsyfunctional Family

Where do I begin? My father was an alcoholic. He was very abusive to my mother and to her kids. Once he chased us up into the attic with an axe. We were running to keep him from hitting us with the axe. In the attic I was crawling over broken glass and dead mice.

My father's friend stopped him from chopping all of us with the axe. There were times when I witnessed him beating my mother and choking her. We would hit him with a chair or anything we could to stop the beatings. My father was vicious when he was drunk and mean when he wasn't.

My mother made a cake to celebrate my father's birthday. Why, I don't know but my father picked me up and threw me into the dining room from the kitchen. Did he think I had anything to do with the cake? I have no idea why this happened. To this day, I am confused with his birthday cake and the wrath I suffered??????

I had a nervous condition dealing with all the drama and violence in our house. So, I started to meditate to deal with the constant violence and sexual abuse. Yes, sexual abuse. My brothers would sexually abuse us. We told my mother about my brothers touching us during the night. She would not do anything. And, when she left the room the boys beat us for telling.

Once my brother said, "Meta, look there's something behind the bed". When I went over to look, one of my older brothers jumped to molest me and I fought him off.

My other blood brother molested my sister who gave birth to a still-born child with physical deformities. This brother still lives in my mother's house as if he hasn't done anything.

For these things I blame my mother. All these years she allowed her sons to molest us and she didn't do anything about it. My oldest brother, who is a step brother, has been to prison for molesting two other girls, ages 10 and 11. He was able to molest these girls by beating their mother who was bed-ridden. After serving 10 years in prison for these molestations, he molested my grandchildren, as well.

My Dsyfunctions

The trip to Inkster wasn't a single incident in my life. I had another friend who was sexually active and perverted. She met some young men at the Museum and enticed them to leave their teacher to have sex with her in different parts of the Museum.

When they looked at me, I said, "…my brothers will beat you up if you try to rape me." One of the young men knew my brothers and said, "…don't touch her, Cuz, her brothers will kick your butt".

Meantime, my friend was having sex in the bathroom stall with one of these young men, as the rest of us waited outside.

Our next adventure together was actually set up on our way home from the Museum. We met a man named Cotazi. We set a date to meet him at his place. I am 15 years old at this time, so we were skipping school to meet at this man's house.

When I arrived, my friend wasn't there. Cotazi said he had sent her for beer. Being young and naïve, I waited. Of course, she didn't return and the results were that I was beaten and told if I screamed no one would hear me. Set up again! This Hispanic man raped me in his apartment on Warren Street, and then walked me home.

Out of the blue, I started to not feel well. This was right after I returned to Detroit. My mother took me to the doctor and I discovered I was pregnant. I told my younger sister I was pregnant. My mother was mad! She kicked me, knocked me down and called me a bitch. She also said don't ever tell your sister anything like that again.

When my son was born my mother wanted to keep him. I didn't want my mother to keep him. She raised molesters and I didn't want my son to be like my brothers.

At age 16, I didn't believe in abortion and didn't want the responsibility of a child. I probably wasn't ready for the responsibility. However, I made the right choice to keep my son. He is a wonderful person; a wonderful father and husband. I am so glad to have my grandchildren. I am a great grandmother because of my original decision to have this son.

When I became pregnant the second time, my mother attempted to put my daughter up for adoption. Had I not asked the Social Worker if I had a choice I would have never known that I could prevent adoption of my daughter. The Social Worker told me I had a choice.

My mother had eleven children, some for my father and many from men she slept around with and brought home. I just didn't want my mother to raise my children. Somehow, I needed to break the cycle. Somehow, I needed to teach my children the right things to do in life.

So, I kept my second child and about a year later became pregnant with the third child. This child's father is a pimp that I fell in love with. He is an older guy that taught me how to survive in the streets and not allow anyone to take advantage of me.

The man I met (the pimp) at age 17 was good to me. My mother didn't like the fact that he was older than me. I don't know why that would make a difference, as I had other boyfriends who were older than me that she allowed me to travel with from time to time.

The first older boyfriend was a truck driver and my mother liked him and was most likely sleeping with him. I came into the house to see him with his shirt off. My mother quickly said, "…it's not what it looks like". In fact, it was exactly what it looked like. I took that as no big deal as I didn't like this man and that was her choice.

My mother loved men who were younger than her. One of her younger boyfriends came to my house and tried to have sex with me. This is not my cup of tea, so I screamed and fought him off. When I told my mother, she said, "you lying bitch", which was the name she called me regularly.

My mother was abusive at times. One day she would hit me and the next day she would want me to go buy bread for the house. I eventually got tired of her hitting, kicking, knocking me down, and stomping me. I felt she was making me the lowest person in the world.

I finally decided to move. How do you tell this mother that you need to leave with your children although you love her? The pimp found a place for me to live and paid the rent. I met him in an after hour joint. This man took care of me. He bought my clothes. He paid the rent. He kept food and shelter for me and my children.

There were women who were turning tricks for him. I was not caught up in that as I was his main woman, of course. I fell in love with him without knowing he was living with one of the prostitutes and she was taking care of him. I was actually just a side piece.

So, since I knew all the prostitutes who were turning tricks, one day I decided to turn a trick. I wasn't experienced or good at this type work and got tricked.

The $50 I made for my attempt at tricking, the trick saw me put the money in the drawer and he stole it back before he left. I knew this was not the career for me. I needed a new career.

Of course, I am still telling lies to get through life. I lost a lot of friends by telling lies. I was also still drinking and getting drunk while trying to be a good mother.

One day I met this young lady named Cat. Cat had been used by men. She was an alcoholic. Cat lived with an abusive man who made her sleep on the floor as his white cat slept in the bed with him. This was a sad, sad situation. I realized God put me here for something better and it was time I stopped drinking and getting drunk.

I saw Cat being dragged in an alley while she was drunk and this is when I decided, "God, you didn't put me here to become like this".

So, I stopped drinking a lot of hard liquor because at the time I didn't want to become an alcoholic. My father was an alcoholic; my brothers were alcoholics and drug addicts; my sisters were addicted to drugs and I had to raise my children. I knew I wanted to be alive to see them have a chance in life.

The first time I got away from the pimp I got on social services and was able to get money and food stamps to get my own place. This man would say to me when I was dependent on him, "I pay the price to be the boss." Well, when I got my place I said, "I pay the price to be the boss." However, I was still allowing people to come around me who didn't mean me or my children any good. These "so called friends" would rip me off or come by to eat my food and I wouldn't see them anymore.

I had to change again. I had to move to a different location and get away from negative people without meeting guys who only wanted sex. I didn't meet too many nice guys who wanted to marry and take care of me and three children.

I met Donald, a police officer who fell in love with me and wanted to marry me. I had a tubal ligation done to avoid having any more children, three was enough.

Donald and I did not get married.

My Daughter, My Daughter

42

What happened to my daughter was beyond my control and the outcome wasn't what I would have expected.

At age 24 I worked in a bar called Sonny Wilson's. A lady, my neighbor, would babysit for me in the Brewster Projects. These projects were full of people on drugs, prostitution and all sorts of crimes. I didn't socialize with a lot of people. This one lady I trusted to babysit for me and her son molested my daughter at age five.

She was aware that her son molested my little girl and allowed it to happen. My other children witnessed it so they knew about the molestation as well. I wasn't aware.

One night when I got home I had a vision it was like a big screen TV and my daughter said this person who I couldn't see his face was fondling her private area. I asked the Lord, why am I seeing something like this? Why was I seeing this nightmare?

My daughter, in her own five year old way, came to try to explain to me what happened to her and I knew it was a warning from God and it wasn't a nightmare.

I took my daughter to Children's Hospital where the doctor examined her vaginal tissues were torn and she had been raped. I talked to the mother of the boy who said, "I'm going to do this and blah, blah, blah."

When confronted, my neighbor lied to the Social Worker that I didn't tell her about the rape, which I know I did. At the time I told her, she denied the allegation saying, "if my son raped your daughter she would be bursted wide open, as he is as big as a man". She refused to accept the fact and refused to ask her son.

I know my daughter was raped because of her story (in her own way) and the other children witnessing the act. The neighbor's son was 12 years old, at the time. I knew then this lady may have been messing with her own son to allow such an ugly thing to happen.

I went to the police department with my daughter. Taking matters into my own hands, I told the police what had taken place and the son was arrested. The police said, "if he did that to your daughter you should kill him."

Since the mother lied, we had to go to court. The doctor testified that my daughter's vagina had been penetrated. The attorney for the boy said she may have hurt herself on a bike or something. This wasn't true. They lied in court. Thank you, Jesus; thank God we won the trial.

Although I don't know the sentencing, this young boy was found guilty of raping my daughter.

God instructed me when we left court to not look around me and don't look back. I had a dream of being at total peace. During the dream I was captured up in His arms and awoke with joy and relief. Although my daughter had been scarred in some way, justice was served and God showed me that there would be joy.

Dreams and Wonders

I am what you may call a dreamer. Yes, I had multiple dreams when I was young. Some I didn't understand and some were very graphic. I recall one dream where it was pitch black outside and people were screaming and running. I looked up in the sky to see a window open and there was Jesus.

I fell down because I didn't have a chance to run. Why should I run? I began to pray, "oh, Jesus, please save me", I began to holler and repent my sins. In this dream planes began to fall from the sky.

Another time I dreamed there were strange animals, some with wings that flew down from the sky. I started to draw pictures on the wall of the dreams I had. Some people would call this paranoia or schizophrenic, but, not me. I call it revelation.

Another dream was that I was in an attic and I see men walking down the street covered from head to toe in some type uniform. As they walked they begin to pick people up from the street and load their bodies into a truck of some type. I don't remember where I was when I had this dream.

I don't remember all dreams, however, here's another. I was lying in bed praising God and thinking about His goodness and where he brought me from. I began to meditate on God's goodness and the next thing I knew I was taken up in my sleep. I had a cool come back down because it was so powerful.

When you get to a place of praising God and knowing that you are in His presence there is no other experience like it.

I have been through so many experiences and decided to go for intercessory prayer. The prayer leader began to prophesy to me that Jesus has been carrying me for a long time. She said I had been complaining about my problems; telling people about what I have been through but Jesus had been with me all along. I looked around and was surrounded by clouds and there was Jesus standing with sandals, and this was winter time.

It was so beautiful. I couldn't see my feet so I knew Jesus had to be carrying me. I also realized I had to stop complaining about issues and problems that I was going through. I had to put aside the pain that I was suffering. At this point, I realized I was an intercessor. Of course, I didn't know anything about interceding for others; I hardly prayed for myself. But God!

I began to pray for other people and my blessings began to come. Things I needed, I didn't have to ask for. God knew I needed a tire one day. I was at a gas station and a stranger came over and said you need a tire. He pulled a tire out of the trunk of his car and put it in my car.

Dreams and wonders!

I said praise the Lord. Thank you. God will use anyone. You do not have to know them. You do not have to be Christian to be blessed. You might be a sinner. You could be a child but he blesses you. So, He blessed me and I am thankful.

I began to reach out to women who were going through similar issues that I was going through, abusive husband, raped children as another daughter was raped by my husband (that comes later in this story).

One day I was with a client and the Holy Spirit instructed me to go to the client, place my hand on her back and demand the demon or spirit to leave her body and she would be healed. I did not do it. At work we were instructed don't go into anyone's home preaching or doing things contrary to the job you are there for. I needed the job to care for my three children and I didn't want to lose my job. So, I didn't intercede as instructed.

A few months later I returned to this client to find she was in a full body cast. I said to her, I was told to pray for you and I didn't. She asked me to pray then and I did. A few months after that, I returned and she was not in the body cast but up doing laundry.

I said, "thank God, thank God." She was happy. I was happy. We had lunch, talked and laughed together. I knew she was Christian as her Priest would come over to deliver communion.

The Farm

I want to back up a bit here. I am the first to admit that my younger days were "hot". I went from one thing in my life to another. There was no controlling what I did and why I did the things I did.

My mother and father had friends who once lived in Inkster. They had property they sold to the City of Inkster to prepare land for Highway 94. So, they had money and moved to Belleville, Michigan. They had two houses built and took in foster kids. My mother sent me there.

This is where I met my cousin for the first time at this foster home. This cousin was taken from her mother because she was neglected. Big Mama and Big Daddy, as they were called, were thought to be nice people. The impression I got when I first met them was that they were nice people.

When I arrived at Belleville I learned the real deal. These weren't nice people at all. Big Mama made us work on the farm to sell the vegetables at the roadside stand. Some children worked with the farm animals. We were beaten.

This is where I discovered I was pregnant from the rape in Detroit, my first pregnancy. I didn't know anything about being pregnant or having a baby because I was 15 years old. I wasn't feeling well and not sleeping a lot.

Big Mama fried onions and left for our breakfast, as she went to town. Fried onions were given to us often to eat and the other food was locked. Only the cook and the twins had a key. Big Mama loved the twins. The twins were her favorite foster children. Well, they unlocked the door and we were able to get food and money from the house, while Big Mama was in town.

We were paid $.25 to work the farm and if we would drink a pop we had to give the $.25 back. Instead of giving Big Mama a quarter, we would go to the corner store or someone's house where they sold candy and other items we might want.

I didn't like eating fresh animals killed on the farm. It actually made me sick to see the animals slaughtered. I would buy cereal and milk or something else to eat when at the store.

Big Mama offered to pay me if I would keep her secret about abusing the foster kids at the farm. I told her I didn't want anything from her and I was going to tell as soon as I could or got the chance to do so.

Naturally, she didn't like me and began to spread lies about me. This woman went so far as to say my mother said I had syphilis. While I was at the farm, I was made to sleep naked since all my clothes were taken. I wasn't able to use the bathroom in the house at night and had to go to the outhouse. I would wait until the next day to pee.

The foster kids at the Farm were not allowed to watch TV at night together. Big Mama thought we were all perverted and wanted to have sex together.

My cousin and I went out with some men to a drive in movie. When we got back to the house, Big Mama was standing at the gate with a gun in her hand threatening to shoot us for going out to the movies.

I visited years later to learn the house burned and Big Mama and Big Daddy were burned with the house. The fire may have been created by some of those children. Was that revenge for their abuse? I don't know…I'm just saying.

Listening

This morning I am full of praises and thanksgiving. God has brought me a long way. One of the times God provided I was on the bus, minding my business, going somewhere (I can't remember exactly where). The Holy Spirit says practice to be quiet. How can I study to be quiet? The Holy Spirit says practice one word. Practice kindness. That's all you need to do is practice this one word. Practice kindness. Practice Love. Practice God's Word.

I have received so much just by listening to the Holy Spirit. One day in traffic I felt the traffic was too much. Within my spirit I heard, "pray for patience". Practice one thing at a time. Today, practice patience. I didn't know patience was something I should pray for but I did and as I did all the traffic seemed to just move along.

I asked God, how are you everywhere? How is it you can see everything? How can you be everywhere at one time? He told me that He is the master designer. God created me. He knows everything about me. He knows the number of hairs on my head. God knows every cell in my body.

God went on to tell me that my life is in a book. God is a designer and I am His child who has been designed. Therefore, He knows every stitch, every pattern and everything about everyone He created.

As a caregiver who has cared for people with HIV, I served women, men, and children. One patient was a sweet little boy whose immune system would go in and out. His father died of HIV/AIDS. The disease was passed on to his mother and to him. To see that child, five years old, pass away while I was taking care of him was devastating.

Married, Another Abuse

I married my first husband at age 36. He was younger than me and delivered Pizzas. About a week before I met him I went to a psyche and she told me I was going to meet this person and was going to get married.

When he came to the door to deliver the pizza I jumped on it really quick and married him. We were married in Toledo, Ohio.

My husband attended New Liberty Apostolic Faith Temple. At this time I really didn't attend church but one day we went to church together. I told him, "…because you are in here don't try to drag me into church because I'm not ready."

One day the Pastor and Elders of the church asked who might be ready to come up and stay all night to tarry. Something right then kicked in that I was ready to start to tarry. (Tarry for those of you who might be unfamiliar, is a process of fasting and praying to receive the Holy Ghost and began to speak in tongues). I tarried that Sunday night, received the Holy Ghost and was baptized on Monday.

Once I received the Holy Ghost I was able to speak in tongues as the Spirit gave orders. I thank God for that was the best thing that ever happened. I was filled with the Holy Spirit and it saved our marriage at least.

Once I was saved I went to church quite often with my husband. We went together with the children and our youngest daughter got saved there as well. My older daughter was having problems because of her diagnosis of chronic schizophrenia after being raped when she was five. She began to do strange things, touching her sister, acting out behavior issues so she received psychiatric care and was in and out of the mental hospital.

I didn't know my husband had mental issues. I got him a job working at a factory. He walked home from the factory one day. This was a long distance out east and we lived on the west side of town. I wondered how did he walk all that way?

This was the first clue that something was wrong. I didn't know what, because I didn't know there were mental issues in his family until later.

I called his family to ask if he had any problems for he had some medication. They said yes, he had medications for mental issues. My husband was not taking this medication. I tried to sneak the medication into his food but he caught on and wouldn't eat thinking that I was giving him the medication.

I found out where his psychiatrist was located. I told him my husband claimed all nine gifts of the spirit and he was acting strangely.

I said I was taking my daughter to see the psychiatrist. That's how I tricked my husband to get him to the psychiatrist. Police Officers were there. My daughter was crying and screaming to the police, "please don't do that." The police took him directly to the Northville Mental Hospital.

This tore me up because I didn't know the person I married. My husband never told me about his mental issues. I was broke. He was in the hospital and I had to find a job to care for my children. I asked the church for help. Some of the deacons helped a little.

My husband could come home every other weekend. He acted strangely when home and did not want to go back. However, he had to go back or once he broke the rules he would not get a chance to come home again.

Finally he was released from the hospital with no medication. I left my daughter at home many times as she was in school off and on due to her mental issues. Something inside said to me don't leave her there because something is going to happen to her. I felt my husband would do something to her. I felt strongly that he would molest her.

Although I had this weird feeling I left for work anyway. This is my older daughter. She and my husband did not get along too well. They fought all the time. He didn't like her and he loved the younger daughter.

Sure enough one day when I returned from work my daughter told me he molested her. I didn't want to believe it since both of them had mental issues and both of them would lie. So, I just didn't know what to do.

He gave my daughter money and they weren't getting along. My sister happened to be there at the time and my daughter told her about what happened between my husband and her. As my daughter told me what he did and how he did it, I was aware that since I didn't do all that freaky stuff he most definitely tried it on her.

My daughter gave a vivid account of what happened and how it happened, including that my husband said to her, "...you know you like it". I knew she was not making accusations, as these were the same words he would say to me. I didn't feel that my daughter had been listening at the door or window to hear our sexual encounters. She explained too well what was done to her and how it was done.

As my daughter is telling what happened to her, the next thing you know he is listening at the door. I asked if there was a problem and that's when I told him he had to leave; he had to go; he had to get out and go live with his mother. I really didn't care where he went but he had to leave my house, immediately.

When I called the church to speak with the Pastor he asked did I know the issue to be true, as my daughter could be lying because of her mental illness. I knew he raped her because she told me the same way when she was five and raped by someone else. I knew my daughter was telling the truth. She told me it wasn't the first time he touched her.

I knew my daughter was telling the truth because of the way she described the sexual encounter and the words my husband used when finished. This was the same posture and position he used with me and the same words when he finished. My daughter could not have made that up.

As I reflect back, personally, I feel his mother and the entire family were kind of strange. But, who am I to judge? I leave them all in God's care.

I had a dream one night that we went to church and he was acting strangely in church talking to a young lady as if it was Saturday Night Live or something similar. In this dream, my husband was hiding in a closet. I don't know exactly what this means, but it was strange.

Well I felt guilty being a Christian and trying to find the truth, I asked him to come back into the house. He said let's pray and fast for God to ask God to help us through this. Next thing I knew we were not praying but he was all over me having sex.

My husband said my daughter was having sex for a long time who knows if she was having sex with other boys. That's when I told him, perhaps she has had sex with other boys but you did this to her. The way she described your actions is actually what you have done to me and it's because you say that's what you like. Get out and don't come back.

He said if you report it to the police I'll go to jail and I'll be back. "No, you will not be coming back here", I said. My daughter threw something at him. She became physical with him so I knew he did something to her for her to act with anger and begin to scream and curse at him.

I took her to the police where they took her statement. He was arrested and his family got him out of jail. He was found guilty and given a sentence of three to 15 years in prison.

Funny, I visited him in prison. I divorced him while he was in prison. The church crucified me constantly. I felt like I was having a dream that I was being nailed to a cross, being crucified, because they disrespected me.

As if what he did to my child wasn't enough; his family tried to run me off the road, and at church his mother wouldn't shake my hand. It wasn't my fault that her son raped my daughter. What could I do?

Deliverance

You may recall my oldest daughter was raped at age 5. Rape seems to run rampant in my family. Rape and attempted rape has caused many situations in my life and the life my children.

It is 6:38 Sunday morning my daughter, Vila, is possessed with an evil spirit she calls her imaginary friend. I believe there was a demon spirit in my house because of so many things happening.

Vila slept with knives and a hammer. The spirit was telling her to do all kinds of things. I believe this trauma was caused by the childhood rape. As she grew older she began to do strange things. She would touch her sister in sexual ways. I didn't take her for help when she was five as I thought maybe she would grow out of it. I didn't get psychiatrist or psychotherapy. As she grew up her behavior worsen that's when I started taking her to a psychologist.

She was diagnosed as schizophrenic, chronic schizophrenia. She was on all types of medications for mental illness. While institutionalized in a teenage facility, Vila was placed in a straight jacket because of her behavior. She would spit on the doctors, break TV's, aggravate the other patients and display unruly behavior. She was very strong and aggressive.

I prayed to God to help me understand and the voice said to me, you reap what you sow. At that moment I forgot what I once was like and God showed me to understand although I did some terrible things while in school, my daughter was doing the same things. She was skipping school. She was constantly in the principal's office for some bad deed. She seemed to always be in trouble.

I said my daughter was possessed by an evil spirit. As I prayed in the spirit one day she came into my room and said the imaginary friend told her to cut my throat with a nail file that was on the dresser. She couldn't do it.

I couldn't understand that my daughter was going to be saved. She was creeping out the window to go out at night. I was so tired, so fed up. I prayed that I didn't go after her. Finally my heart and mind knew God heard me. I opened the door and commanded Satan to get out of my house, in the name of Jesus.

Then I was in church praying in the spirit when a deacon tapped me on the shoulder. I went to the back of the church, and there was my daughter praying in tongues, crying and thanking God.

I was so thankful that God had taken over. He said he would deliver my daughter from mental illness. The next day my daughter was in the kitchen cooking dinner. She was back to her normal self. Oh, my God. It was a miracle. God delivered her from the demon inside.

Back to Detroit

There are times when you go back. You have to go back to move forward. My mother wanted me to come and live with her again. Of course, I didn't want to live with her because in the past this was not a pleasant time. My mother beat me in front of my children until I was 19 years old.

As my mother attempted to beat me at one point, my daughter stuck her foot out and tripped her, causing her to stumble. This was so that I would avoid the beating my mother was giving at the time.

At age 19 my mother's boyfriend, John, asked her to put me out. I moved into my own place down the street. This place was full of mice or rats that ran through the walls. You could hear them running all night.

I would sit up, like a cat, waiting to trap them as they ran out of their hiding places. I would sit in the closet to grab them by the tail with a pair of pliers. Then take them into the kitchen and put the rat under hot water until dead.

One day as I was putting the trash out I saw a rat. The rat turned and looked at me. Knowing he was alive I ran inside and got a pot of hot water and threw on the rat. The rat jumped straight up and ran under the steps. That scared the crap out of me. I don't know if he lived or went away to die.

Parent Dysfunctions

My entire childhood wasn't on getting beat up and spanking. I had some good times. I can remember going to Belle Isle Park chilling, going to Boblo Boat and Edgewater Park, with my siblings.

We had such nice times there with friends doing things I can remember as good times, good things. Batman X. Some of those memorable times was going out drinking with my father. We would go to his friend's house where others were drinking and having fun.

My father and I had been drinking. He stopped and tried to kiss me. I don't know why but he tried to kiss me in my mouth, and, I didn't like that at all. There was no way I was going to allow him to kiss me, especially on my lips. That was out of the question. My father never tried that move again.

I know this behavior is just passed down through our family. It's like a grave vine or any other vine. It is hard to kill a grave vine. Unless the root of the vine is killed, the vine can grow to strangle anything to which it attaches, killing off or stunting the growth of the tree, flower, bush or whatever it is attached..

I told my father don't ever try that again. He was drunk and I was drunk, but no way. I believe family members have been molested during their lives. I don't know who molested who. I probably will never know the answers for everyone since both my parents are now dead. My father died, I believe of cancer, at age 62. My mother died of a heart attack and some other complications.

My father stopped drinking before he died and we grew closer in relationship. I love my father.

Of course, when my mother passed away I didn't feel anything. Before she passed she asked me to take her to the hospital and I didn't. I asked my brother to take her and that's where she died in the hospital.

I didn't cry when she died. I couldn't feel anything because I was glad finally she was gone and I don't have to put up with her anymore. I will not be disrespected any longer. She told the other kids that I was on drugs. She did a lot of things that most mothers wouldn't do to their children.

My mother separated us. She was a trouble maker who constantly did things to cause friction within our family.

You should know that I loved her in my own way, but, it's a blessing that she is gone. I feel she was so bad for me. She told me she didn't love me. When I tried to hug her she pushed me away and didn't want me to hug her.

My mother acted as if I was poison. She treated my children like dogs. I had a dream before I moved back with my mother that I was fighting with the devil. When I moved back with her that's exactly what I was doing, fighting the devil.

I came home from work and everything was sitting on the lawn. I asked what was going on and was told my mother was being evicted because she had not paid a roofing bill. My mother did not pay her bills. She was being evicted once again.

When I asked what I could do to stop the eviction. The white man gave me a number to call. I made arrangements to pay the $100 dollars I had, as I could not come up with $1,000 just like that. The men stopped taking furniture out of the house as I went to pay the bill and make arrangements to catch up the back payments. My mother had neglected to pay bills since I was a child.

At the Apostolic Faith Temple I was around a lot of mothers of the church. After church we would go to their house and have dinner. These sisters always prepared great dinners, fried chicken, collard greens and all the home cooking.

When my mother passed, God told me that this one particular mother in the church would be my mother. I thought, wow, God will give me someone to talk with, someone to be my mother. I was so thankful that He was thinking about my life.

I thank God for saving me. There were times I thought I wasn't going to be saved and surely I was going to hell because of all the things hanging over my head. God reached down to save me when I thought I was just the scum of the earth, a worm of the earth, not worthy of His presence.

I thank God so much for being that father in my life that I didn't have and being my brother, my doctor, my everything. My life in the church is a spiritual hospital. I thank God for that.

Second Time Around

My second husband I met at the same church. I have been going to Apostolic Faith Temple for many years. This man was in prison for 10 years. I started to see him out of loneliness. Perhaps because I was always molested, it was easy to mistake love with sex.

We moved in together with my children at the time. My youngest daughter, Susie, was still at home. I had a roommate in my house. She was a Christian whose brother was a Pastor and she was a church going person, so I took her in as a roommate.

She was a recovering drug addict but began to hang around with the same people and started to use drugs again. I didn't want this lifestyle in my house and asked her to move. She felt she didn't want to move and threatened me that she was not going to move.

Sam helped me get her out of the house. My daughter Susie became pregnant. Due to my sleep apnea I am a sound sleeper and boys were sneaking into the house to be with Susie without my knowing. I tried to get Susie to go to the pregnancy center where they could help her to continue her education and learn to take care of her baby. She didn't want to go.

So, Susie was at the house when Sam and I moved together. Her older sister, Vila, was at the mental hospital now for more than a year. One day I asked Susie to do the dishes. Her response was when she was ready to do them.

As a result of this incident, Susie called my sister, Ann, who was a drug user and moved with her. I packed all her clothes and had them ready for the move, since she did not want to obey my rules. I did not want to be responsible for taking care of her baby, since she was only 16 years old.

Sam and I were married by my Uncle, the Preacher. We had a few friends over later for a reception. Married for six years, we bought a house together on the east side of Detroit.

Then Sam became violent towards me. We argued about money and once he knocked me down and began to kick me. I knew then that I was living with a devil. Our sex life was horrible because he slept with men in prison. He carried a picture in his wallet of the white man, who was his lover, in prison.

At this point, Sam wants me to do things that are not only uncomfortable to me but also unclean. Because I didn't do those things he said prostitutes were better than me. Sam also said my body was disgusting.

I packed my things and left. He, of course, came to me and promised he would not beat me anymore and he wasn't going to put his hands on me anymore. So, I moved back.

That was a big mistake. He continued. One day he put a knife at my throat and said, "bitch, I should kill you." This was because I opened a separate bank account to have escape money knowing what I know from past relationships.

Sam would often say if you hang around the barbershop long enough sooner or later you will get a haircut. Well, Sam was hanging around the drug users he formerly was with and started using drugs again.

One day he came home high and announced, "you ain't seen nothing yet." I hadn't seen what was about to happen. He disappeared one day and didn't come back for days. I soon learned he was at a crack house.

When he returned he looked so strange. It was terrifying to me. There were times I got him from his Uncle's house, the crack house, and brought him home. He continued to use crack. At home he was violent.

I went to drug treatment with him. I went to Al-Anon with him. Nothing helped. I went to abused women centers. I went to psychotherapist. I saw psychiatrist to try to find out why this is happening to me.

I was told it was in the man I was married to and that none of these issues with Sam's drug abuse and physical violence was my fault.

Before this nightmare was over, Sam tried to commit suicide while driving with my daughter in the car. He also took my other daughter's car, attempted to sell the car and left her on the curbside crying.

At this point I felt like driving into a brick wall and killing myself. Something took over and said you are not going to kill yourself.

I thank God that I didn't kill myself, However, I feel horrible that he abused my child and abused me for six years. Sam asked me one day, you aren't going to leave again are you? I said no.

Then, one day I packed all my belonging in the car, took off and never went back. I took all my money out of the bank, found a lawyer and divorced him.

This was a dramatic time. I was stalked. I got a protective order against him. This was the only way I could be free from Sam's abuse.

A Complete Shift

Working as a Nursing Assistant I went with my cousin to a Sagittarius party at Queens and Kings Club. That's where I met my present husband.

This man is nice and charming. He lied that he was a cook because he can't cook a thing. However, other than that he is a good person. I prayed that the Lord would send me a husband better than the ones I had before.

We have now been together for 21 years. One time he said some ugly things to me and I straightened that out right away. I made it clear that I had been in so many abusive relationships and suffered so much abuse that I would no longer stand for any abuse. At this point, I made it clear that I would allow no one to speak to me any kind of way in the name of Jesus. I knocked that stuff off right away.

Now for the 21 years we have been together he has never put his hands to hit me or speak to me in an abusive or downgrading manner.

So many things in my life have changed and I thank God. I came through the fire. I have forgiven those past relationships. I actually went to see people to let them know they were forgiven.

I cannot carry that baggage into my new life. Old things are passed away and behold all things have become new.

It was necessary for me to leave that baggage and forgive those men for mistreating me. This is the lesson I learned by being married to my present husband. I just thank God that He didn't give up on me. God never gave up on me even when I gave up on God.

I have backslidden in marriages. I have chosen men in my life that caused traumatic things to happen. I went through sexual abuse and rape. I introduced alcohol into my life and my family. I chose the wrong path in life often times. I picked the wrong people in my life. But, I just thank God for not giving up on me.

It's like having a child where you hold the child with a leash to keep up with the child or to keep the child from getting away. You hold the leash close. That's what God does with His children. He keeps us close with his leash. He will let the leash out and pull it back when you have gone too far.

I could have been dead a long time ago with all the things that were happening to me. But I thank God because he never let me go. God gives you tests and trials like basic training. He is getting you ready for the battle to come.

There was a time when God gave me a test. I was caring for a patient and her left hand would not open. The Holy Spirit spoke to me and said when your left hand offends you, cut it off. The meaning of this was that anything that hinders you from being with God, let it go...cut it off. I thank the Holy Spirit for that lesson.

I thank God for bringing me to Orlando, FL and Pastor Riva Tims. I feel so blessed. I have met a lot of wonderful people who are my brothers and sisters in God. I thank God for the job that I have to help seniors and spread the love of God that's inside me.

God gave me this job that isn't a lot of money but it's caring for people. My boss is so nice. She treats me kind so I know God made her for me.

I want everyone to know that whatever you are going through in life or, whatever you have been through in life—there's a way out.

There's a way of escape and it's Jesus. I thank God for making a way for my escape. Yes, Jesus is good. He will not put things on you that you cannot bear. I will look back and say at times when I am going through something in life, I can bear this too.

When you think you cannot bear life, read this book. If I can get through all of this, so can you. The Lord has blessed me with 13 grandchildren, nine great-grandchildren and one on the way. My granddaughters are in college. They are getting degrees. My grandson is in the Army in Germany. I have a granddaughter who is also in the Army in Kentucky. I have so much to be proud of and so much to thank God for bringing me from where I was to where I am today.

My son will be 50 next year and he has such a wonderful family. My grandchildren are all wonderful.

I am thankful for where God has brought me but most of all I am thankful for where He's taking me!